BANGLAR BOW (BENGALI BRIDE)

SHANTI DEODHARI

Bloomington, IN  Milton Keynes, UK

AuthorHouse™
1663 Liberty Drive, Suite 200
Bloomington, IN 47403
www.authorhouse.com
Phone: 1-800-839-8640

AuthorHouse™ UK Ltd.
500 Avebury Boulevard
Central Milton Keynes, MK9 2BE
www.authorhouse.co.uk
Phone: 08001974150

First published by AuthorHouse 2/6/2007

ISBN: 978-1-4259-8155-6 (sc)

Printed in the United States of America
Bloomington, Indiana

This book is printed on acid-free paper.

ACKNOWLEDGEMENT

I would like to thank my family; the women in Village Borkapon, Moulvi Bazar for their encouragement to publish this little book and Mohammed Mahmud for taking me to his country and sharing his experiences.

I would like to thank Chrissy Lacey from Inverness for the editing and support.

I would also like to thank Dr. John Mayberry for his inspiration and support to publish this book that may benefit public and private sector workers in their diversity training.

CONTENTS

MONAY PORAW

At this time of my parting, wish me good luck, my friends! The sky is flushed with the dawn and my path lies beautiful.

Ask not what I have with me to take there. I start on my journey with empty hands and expectant heart.

I shall put on my wedding garland. Mine is not the red-brown dress of the traveller, and though there are dangers on the way I have no fear in my mind.

The evening star will come out when my voyage is done and the plaintive notes of the twilight melodies be struck up from the King's gateway.

Gitanjali (Rabindranath Tagore)

After careful preparations and major decisions about what to pack in our suitcases, we were finally ready to leave! I found it very difficult to part company with our two dobermans, Kalia and Nitu but was assured by our friend Mr. Willie Allan that they would be well taken care of, as they were staying in our house and not going to the kennels. We bade farewell to our neighbours and friends.

It was almost one'o clock in the morning. We left our home in Balloch, Inverness, Scotland; it was a cold September morning and the sky was clear.

Driving for approximately ten hours, we decided to visit a few of our relatives in Birmingham, Coventry and London, then to Horndean, Hampshire where we stayed for few days. It was very cold and we were looking forward to the hot climate in Bangladesh.

Our flight B.A. 747 left London, Heathrow on 30th September 1991 at 10.50 in the evening for Zia International Airport, Dhaka, Bangladesh. After we had checked in and were left with only two pieces of hand luggage, we made our way to the immigration, then did some shopping in the duty free shop.

After we boarded the aircraft, we made ourselves comfortable and were ready for our long cruise. The flight was delayed for about thirty minutes - a thirteen hour journey ahead and sitting very relaxed I was remembering when I first came to Britain.

I came to Britain in the early 70's to pursue my Nursing career. I had started my Orthopaedic Nursing training at St. Vincent's Orthopaedic Hospital, Eastcote, Pinner, Middlesex, where I stayed for two years. It was very pleasant working there. It was a Hospital managed by Sisters of Charity. They took care of us as many girls were from overseas. There were no male student nurses, except one Charge Nurse in the male ward. I was an extremely shy person and my first ward was the male ward. Many a time I wished the floor could have opened and I could have disappeared into the ground because I had my leg pulled by these men. Another girl, Janet Smith and I were almost bullied by the patients. It took us a long time to overcome our shyness. We progressed on to different wards and I was seconded to Hillingdon Hospital, Uxbridge, for nine weeks, to another male Orthopaedic ward! Because of my shyness I had very few friends. Two years later, I went to The Royal Hospital, Richmond, Surrey to pursue my General Nursing training, because although I had gained my Orthopaedic Nursing Certificate I could not practice in the other wards as a qualified nurse but only as a nursing assistant.

It was great fun working at The Royal Hospital, and our comings and goings to and from the Nurses' Home were not so restricted as previously. I was still shy but not as before. My training finished after one year as I was pre - trained. I remained for six months in the Private Ward and then went to work at The Middlesex Hospital, London. It meant more responsibility and I loved it. I worked in the Orthopaedic ward as a Staff Nurse and after eighteen months worked in the Private Wing of the same-Hospital.

During my time in London I went out regularly with Babul. I had met him at a social gathering. I went home approximately every two years. I loved going home, I loved my family, I would be spoilt by them!

It meant taking a number of presents because I had four sisters and two brothers. It was very difficult to take gifts for my aunts and uncles as I had quite a number of them.

The first time I had left home my farewell party was huge. It was like a wedding party. A lot of the guests were worried that I was incapable of taking care of myself, as I was fragile and shy and weighed only about six and a half stones. I was always ill as a child and seemed to pick up any illnesses that were circulating at the time. My parents were also worried about me. I kept re-assuring everyone that I would be fine and there was nothing they could have done for me to change my mind. I felt this was my vocation in life.

My father was the only bread winner in the family and I felt I had to help the family, although we were comfortable financially and in a better position than most families. It was time for changes in Guyana at that period. Because there were more women than men, quite a number of girls about our age had also left the country. We were scattered all over the globe and became of tremendous help to our folks. My sister Lita joined me in Britain in the mid - 70's and there were many other members of other families migrating overseas.

I was proud to have had my younger sister with me, she lived in another Nurses' Home in the country and became a Nurse but hated every moment of it! We visited each other once every week and fought and laughed like we did when we were kids. It was great! We visited our aunt and uncle in W. Germany every year and it was our first home in Europe. We loved it there. Our uncle and aunt were good to us.

It was very emotional for both of us when we left home, because we had left our parents, grandparents, sisters and brothers, and uncles and aunts. We were close to our relatives and it was heart breaking to leave our people and our country of Guyana.

Our childhood experiences were good and we had great fun because we were a large family but came in sets of three. We always had guests at our home in Fyrish (the name of the place where I was brought up in Guyana) Our relatives would suddenly appear and of course were given full board and lodging;

few of my father's cousins stayed with us to further their education because transport was poor where they lived.

When people were staying, we had to share our beds, often with old aunts or grandmothers - sometimes we slept on the floor because they complained we kicked them on our sleep! We loved them to stay with us because of the numerous stories they told and we especially liked the ghost stories. We had a radio, but no one I knew had a television. We went to the local cinema to see alll the latest Hindi Indian Films (English Subtitles) but we had to be accompanied by an elder. Although we were encouraged to read a lot, I hated reading. I spent most of my childhood painting (watercolour). I hated the kitchen and only cooked one meal in my adolescent life. We always had another lady to help my mother with the household chores and she gave some of the clothes to another lady who managed a laundry service. As I have said, in our family we came in sets of three. I was the middle one of three girls and we were very fussy if our clothes were not washed and ironed to our satisfaction, so most of the time my older sister and I did our school uniforms. There would be no creases and the pleats on our skirts would remain exactly as sewn by our seamstress mother. She sewed all our clothes and she was excellent at sewing. We seldom bought ready - made clothes although occasionally I went around the shops with my older sister. I stayed at home most of the time with my mother but my older sister was always out with her friends or at the shops. She bought the materials for my mother to make into dresses - the three of us wore the same styles and same colour of dresses. My mother was very generous with laces and ribbons! I had long hair and could never have managed to comb or brush it without my mother's help. My mother did my hair until I left home to migrate to Britain.

When I was growing up in Guyana, we had our own small family business and after school hours (after four in the afternoon) we had to help in our factory, to tie the food carriers in bundles of threes', sixes' or twelves'. My father had about forty men working for him, making food carriers, buckets and various other household products from aluminium and galvanised sheets. Because there were no plastic household goods sold, we supplied the whole country with either galvanised or aluminium products. We had the only Tinware Factory in Guyana and were proud of it. We also made chowmein and vermercelli noodles in another part of our factory. It was quite large and we had all the huge machinery for various jobs.

Behind our factory we had a large pond where we had our own supply of fishes. My father bought small fishes, like Tilapia, Carp, and other varieties and allowed them to grow to a fair size and then we would use our hooks to catch them. They made good meals for us! The water in the pool was fairly clean because every month my father would pump the water into the stream at the back and re - dig the pool with the help from other men and then filled it from the stream; the fishes were deposited into a barrel of water until the pool was ready for their return.

I enjoyed fishing. Around our pond were coconut palm trees, so it meant we could sit under the trees and catch our fishes without getting too burnt from the scorching sun! There was a group of us, most of the time my younger sister, myself and a couple of the neighbours' children. Sometimes on Sundays if we did any fishing we made our own little barbecue and cooked a meal for us kids. We called it "all in one" which meant cooking rice, black eye peas, vegetables and the poor little fishes caught, all together in the same pot! Everyone of us brought something from our mother's kitchen. Most of the days were hot and humid and when it rained, usually without warning, it poured. As a child I used to enjoy watching our pond fill with the rain water. We always had thunderstorms which were quite scary. Once we had an earth tremor. Apparently Brazil was hit by an earthquake in the late '60's and it affected us about 2 o'clock in the morning and my father woke everyone of us to experience the tremor. I can still remember it clearly.

Guyana is about 83,000 square miles and has a population of approximately 900,000 people. It is 6 ft. below sea level and is susceptible to floods, but is protected by sea - walls. It is North East of South America near to the Atlantic Ocean. Although it is a South American country it is more Carribean because Guyana is part of the Carribean Community. The language is English (some of the people speak Patwa English – broken English) because Guyana was British Guiana until 1966 when it became an independent country. The President just now is Dr. Cheddi Jagan. Guyana, like most of the other third world countries has suffered tremendous debt problems and is still a developing country. Dr. Jagan predecessors fought hard to save the economic growth of the country.

Guyana is a multi - racial society. There are more Indo -Guyanese (our forefathers were from India) than any other races. There were more Hindus than any other Religions. Although I was born a Hindu, (Bramhin by birth - the caste system slowly faded as people integrated and with the acceptance of some of the elders it was tolerable) I was brought up as a Christadelphian, our Ministers having come from Great Britain. I never missed Sunday school ; every Sunday we did Bible studies, in our neighbours' upstairs - sitting room. I went to Bible studies until I was seventeen years old and every year we were given tests from the Bible and at Christmas all the parents were invited from all the different Sunday Schools to attend the Christmas play, held at the big Church in New Amsterdam (which is the second largest town in Guyana). At the end of the play prizes were awarded to the best students and I was always proud to hold a second place because my eldest sister took the first place every year.

And now, all these years later, I realised I was on my way to Bangladesh where the Religion was mostly Muslim. I had had some insight into some of the customs of the Moslem Community as Guyana had a number of people who were Moslems.

My in - laws were Moslems and during my courting days with Babul, he was very shy to take me to his house because it was unacceptable to his parents that he should be friendly with a girl who was not of their Religion. But their attitude softened over the years, particularly after he had been in hospital for an operation. His parents were also returning to their country for a year. We were living in London at that time and I was working as an Agency Nurse in various London Hospitals and Clinics.

Babul always worked in Restaurants (Indian or English) because he did not have an opportunity to complete his studies. When his parents emigrated to Great Britain in the late '60's they stayed at an uncle's residence in Coventry until they moved to London.

Babul had only two brothers in comparison to my large family. He was also the middle of three brothers. We were both busy in our jobs because he was working extra hours so he could purchase his own Restaurant which he eventually did. He was partner in an Indian Restaurant in Seven Sisters, London and then moved to the countryside in East Wittering, W. Sussex. I was still working as a Nurse when we eventually bought our first home in East Wittering. It was beautiful by the sea and it was always busy in the summer and quiet in the winter months, because it was a holiday resort. At nights we could hear the lashing of the waves against the shore. It was tranquil and peaceful. We enjoyed living there. I had an excellent job working in the Accident and Emergency Department at St. Richard's Hospital ; Chichester. After three years we decided to move to somewhere very different and Babul found a successful business in Inverness, Scotland. It was very traumatic because we had my younger brother-in-law, mother-in-law and father-in-law, and acquired a large boisterous Doberman. The dog gave us a hard time because it was our first dog and he was hyperactive. He was uncontrollable! If the front door was open he would run, then wait for us - when we reached him he would do another half-mile! By the time we caught him we were exhausted and he was still full of energy! And it involved the entire family trying to catch him! He is not as active now as he was before, but although he is nine years old, he can be a handful at times! He is nearly eight stones. But we have grown to love him more for his naughtiness!

It was difficult to take care of Kalia (the Doberman) but he had excellent care. I was at work and also Babul worked locally in his own Indian Restaurant. My mother-in-law and father-in-law were left with the dog whilst we were at work. Their English was imperfect but the dog understood whatever commands were made. It was difficult for my in-laws to live in the same house with a dog because in most third world countries dogs are prohibited from entering the house. Also in most Religions animals are forbidden to stay in the house. Animals are treated differently because people are the number one priority and if one does own a good breed of dog then it is kept in a kennel otherwise it is left to wander around the streets. The owners are not too worried about the safety of their dogs.

In my own country my father always had the best of breeds but they were kept outside the house - in the kennels during the day and at nights in our Factory for Security reasons. We did not play, nor were we in any physical contact with the dogs as we are now with our two. But we loved our dogs and stood outside the kennels and spoke to them. We always had someone else to take care of the dogs. In our country it was different because if one was financially secure the odd jobs were done without any physical strain. I felt comfortable at home in my country because I never knew about the odd jobs, but they were done!

I found it hard at times when I was living in East Wittering because after work I had the household chores to do. The cooking was difficult because as I mentioned earlier I had only cooked one meal whilst

I was at home in Guyana but now I had to cook for my in-laws as well as ourselves. It was expected that I should do the various chores. I hated cooking and preferred to do other jobs.

I was expected to wear the sari as it was traditional for the Bengali bride to do so but I continued to wear European clothes I was accustomed to and wore the sari occasionally.

Our marriage was not traditional ; we went to a Registry office and signed the necessary papers followed by a meal. We kept our marriage a secret and did not tell our folks because we did not want a traditional wedding. But I would have loved to have had a traditional wedding, wearing the beautiful red sari and decorated in gold jewellery, with my hands and feet painted in different patterns with henna paint. I very much wished for the traditional Indian wedding. But we kept our love affair and marriage simple and quiet. We had many ups and downs during the period my in-laws were living with us because of the language barrier between us. I could not speak any Bengali and their English was poor but we tried to communicate through sign language. It was very trying at times, especially after a hard day's work at the Hospital.

We sold our three-bedroomed terraced house in East Wittering in the early '80's and moved temporarily to Invergordon until we found another house nearer to Inverness, Scotland. Eventually we bought a house in Balloch about six miles from Inverness. It was beautiful and very quiet. I stayed at home and took care of my husband and his younger brother who attended the local Academy School. My mother-in-law and father-in-law returned to their country Bangladesh and visited us after a couple of years for a short period. They felt the climate would be more suitable to them in Bangldesh.

We decided it was time for another dog and bought Nitu another Doberman from a litter of eleven puppies belonging to a gentleman in Inverness. Her brother and herself were the last to remain from the pack. Nitu was already four months old when we brought her home in comparison to Kalia who was nine weeks old and a gorgeous puppy. Nitu was shy and followed me most of the time. She went to a training school in Inverness and did well, quite unlike Kalia who went to a training school in Chichester and never stopped "winding" and we were told not to take him there again as he was disrupting the class.

But after getting settled in Balloch, suddenly I found myself alone. My husband was busy at the Restaurant all the time and did not return home until the early hours of the morning. Most nights I sat waiting for him to return home and gave him a little snack before we retired to bed. He was partner at The Raja Indian Restaurant and also partner at the Rose of Bengal. Both restaurants were in the town which was convenient for him because our new home was very near, but I worried that our relationship was suffering as his business prospered.

In 1986 I took my husband to my country Guyana for a short holiday and I remained for four weeks whilst he had returned to Scotland after seventeen days. I returned with my youngest sister Arnica who decided to remain with us for a short while and go to Inverness College. Our three - bedroomed bungalow was full and my younger brother-in-law Jahangir was always busy with his friends. My sister and myself were alone in the evenings because my husband was always at work. Seldom did I see him. I spent most of my time entertaining guests and took care of the garden and all the household chores as I was unemployed. My husband felt it was time for me to retire and remain in the house. At first I was devastated as I felt I should have continued working as a Nurse but I had worked harder in the home. I found my lifestyle was being changed to suit everyone else's agenda. My husband had became irritable and everyone had to be careful when speaking to him. He was obviously overworking and all the anxieties and fears were thrown in our directions. We seldom went on outings because he was too busy. We were extremely lucky to go twice yearly to the cinema and perhaps once yearly to London for few days. I hardly saw him and our communication was deteriorating slowly over the years. Our marriage was gradually fading but we stayed together because we felt we had gone against our parents' wishes in marrying. My husband's younger brother Jahangir left home when he was nineteen years old and started to work in his brother's restaurant part-time and attended full time College during the day. My younger sister moved away from home and found employment elsewhere. We were alone but always had guests.

I found myself alone many times but kept busy in the garden in the summer. I took up painting (watercolour) I had enjoyed as a child. Later I became a member of the Art Society in Inverness and exhibited my work every summer. I tried to keep myself busy and borrowed many books from the local Library. I also knitted sometimes. I had few friends Mrs.

Mary Rose and Miss Ann Kennedy both in their late seventies were good companions.

I have been so busy recapturing my thoughts that I had almost forgotten I was in an Aircraft. This was my first visit to Bangladesh as my husband and his relations had lived in Britain most of their lives. I was the foreign Banglar Bow because my husband's older brother was married to his first cousin from Bangladesh. My in-laws were waiting for us at their home in Moulvi Bazar, Bangladesh. I was also looking forward to visiting the plot of land my husband had bought for his orphanage. To build an orphanage in his native land had been his dream for many years. And now, Bombay! It did not register in my brain that I was actually in India!

Soon we were on our way to Dhaka, Bangladesh (a land of many waters) After about two hours we arrived at Zia International Airport, Dhaka - 1st October 1991, about 4 o'clock in the afternoon.

Hustling through mendicants and poverty with the consequent stench, we were taken to our relatives' house Mr. & Mrs. Shafiq Ur Rahman made us very comfortable. It was almost dusk and it was still hot and humid!

Dhaka is a city of mosques and shrines. It is a city with avenues of trees, skyscraper buildings and people of more or less the same colour - brown-skinned. It is a mixture of wealth and poverty. I have never seen so many people in my life! Driving through the streets was a horrendous experience. Drivers in buses and cars used their horns to get their paths clear. The rickshaws outnumbered the cars. The bells of the rickshaws were constantly ringing and the drivers shouting. Many times I felt we were about to have an accident, as our chauffeur drove through large and narrow roads to take us to our first stop.

Having rested for one night in Dhaka the following morning, after a large breakfast, we bade farewell to our hostess. Our host took us to the station. The sun was out ; it was only eight o' clock in the morning and I was dreading the heat!

We were on our way to Moulvi Bazar, Sylhet, my husband's birth place and family residence.

At Kamplapur station, Dhaka, our luggage was taken out from the car and fetched by a porter (coolie) a rather largely built dark-skinned man, who put the two suitcases on his thickly padded head and carried the other hand luggage in one hand to the carriage in the train. With a great deal of hesitancy he accepted a small fee for carrying the luggage.

Our train left promptly at 8:40 a.m for Sri Mongol. We shared our carriage with another family of three. Of course, it was first class but not what I had expected!

The seats were double bunks and we were able to close the top bunks, so we had enough space. The suitcases were put under the seats. The seats were quite dusty and a few areas torn. They were made from a plastic material.

The two windows were covered with nets for protection from dust and insects. They were double windows and between them, in the carriage, was a small shelf. The floor was wooden but clean. We were privileged to have a fan. The carriage was like a small room and there were lights that were out of order.

As the train left Kamplapur station, similiar to Victoria station, in London, England the homeless were visibly seen, with make shift - tents for homes resulting in poor hygiene. The stench along the railway was unbearable. With the added heat it was uncomfortable, but we all need experience in life and this was mine!

As the train lingered along its line we could see the people cooking and washing their utensils and clothes. There were also several markets. The train stopped at a few places where there were greasy looking young and old men, selling their fruits and cigarretes. They forced their items through the windows of the train for us to buy and were appealing to us to buy whatever they were selling. They were clad in torn clothes and stank of sweat. There were also beggars crying "Allah Bhikari" meaning "In God's name help the beggar". So how could one refuse if one is a first time visitor ? We quickly learnt from the family seated opposite to us to read our newspapers, which were wide enough to hide our faces! How many bhikaris can one help!

I was very thirsty but could not get a cool drink to buy. We were served with a snack of bread, egg and tea and a jug of water was left on our table. I was told the snack was included in the price of the ticket as we were travelling first class. I was too afraid to eat or drink anything because of the poor hygiene, quite unlike the family seated opposite us. They swallowed everything in no time! Hungry perhaps! I wanted to have a good journey. We exchanged very little conversation with them during our journey.

As we left the city and travelled towards the countryside, there were no more homeless people living alongside the railway. We could see the ricefields and beautiful trees and houses. There were now different shades of green, from olive to prussian green. The sky was blue. After about five hours, we reached Sri Mongol, a small busy countryside station, with people hustling and bustling, trying to sell their items to us. We were greeted by a few relatives and made our way to Moulvi Bazar, by a mini-bus. By this time, about 2 o'clock in the afternoon, the heat was penetrating our bones and we had to stop for cool drinks. We were going to Moulvi Bazar, Village Borkapon, about twelve miles from Sri Mongol.

The greenery on both sides of the bumpy roads was astonshing and there were a couple of rivers that meandered through the ricefields and trees. It was the perfect countryside. Moulvi Bazar has approximately eight hundred thousand people and is a beautiful country setting for a painting.

Having arrived in Village Borkapon, we were greeted by my mother-in-law, Mrs. T. Nessa. She took us into the house where my father-in-law, Mr. Alla Miah, was waiting along with other relatives and friends, who welcomed us. It was a highly emotional time!

BANGLAR BOW

Banglar Bow or the Bengali bride has much to do. She is the Ma and Bhap (Mother and Father) of her home. She has to look after her home but is never alone. Privacy is limited.

She is married, sometimes at thirteen or fourteen years old and is merely a child herself. She is moulded into a woman by her in-laws (shashuri). It is always traditional for her to move in with her husband's relations. Her task is a heavy burden at times. If her in-laws are reasonably financially secure, she is one of the fortunate ones to have a servant to do most of the cooking and other household chores. Soon she is expected by her in-laws to have her children. (If there is an infertility problem, it can result in one or more nervous breakdown) There is no waiting or getting to know her husband.

It is very rare for her to have been courted by her husband before marriage and pre-marital sex is prohibited. Nearly all the marriages are arranged by the brides' and grooms' parents.

In most arranged marriages the bride and bridegroom are relatives, for example, first cousins marry each other. They grow to love each other afterwards. Sometimes the bridegroom has not seen the bride until the wedding day after the marriage ceremony is over. When they are in the bedroom, he gently lifts the veil and then surprise! a beautiful (shondori) bride, which is not always the case. But beauty is not everything in an arranged marriage.

The most important part in an arranged marriage is her duties in the house, to cook, clean and look after her husband's parents, brothers and sisters ; if there are any. Because of illiteracy cleanliness is not her first priority.

Balobasha or love comes later. Romance climbs up the ladder. One can grow to love another and in most of these arranged Bengali marriages, it is customary to fall in love later. It is very rare to have divorces, because it is considered a taboo.

As the reader is aware some moslem men are enticed to have more than one wife. So a man has choices if the first marriage fails.

Most of the girls are from poor families and therefore are subjected to abuse. The girl has no choice but to remain with the in-laws. She feels she has food and shelter and more or less has to accept the other wife or wives.

Banglar Bow does feel jealous at times of the other wives but it seems, she is made to feel grateful-she is provided with full board and lodging. Her life continues, carrying out the various household chores. Because of poverty, she has to remain with the in-laws. But if her parents are financially secure she could return to them and divorce her husband. (Most couples are not divorced because of young children). It often creates housing problems if she does move home again with her parents as there are younger or older brothers and sisters with their families.

Before Banglar Bow is married she wears shalwar kameez, tight fitting trousers followed by a baggy fitting top that falls over the knees mid-calf area. A shawl is thrown loosely around the neck, to cover the breasts (Oolna).

Sari is a traditional dress. It is about five to six yards long and can be very attractive. Saris come in all different colours and can be plain or patterned and are worn with a tight fitting blouse, a long petticoat to hold it in place as it is wrapped around the waist once, then four or five pleats are formed to hang loosely infront. The remaining paloo or end piece, about one and a half yards, is thrown around the left shoulder and around the right like a shawl, meeting over the breast - area (optional as it could be left hanging over the left shoulder) The new bride is mostly in red attire. This is the most enjoyable time to wear all the different colours because when she becomes a widow Banglar Bow has to wear plain white saris. She is always in multi-coloured dress wear because she is pampered by the relatives and given new saris as gifts, every now and then.

There are no special styles to her hair. It is only combed and tied back, with sometimes oil applied. The girls' faces are beautiful and do not require make-up.

On the marriage day Banglar bow is covered in (shuna) gold jewellery. After a few days getting accustomed in the inlaw's home, she locks away her precious jewels and wears multicoloured glass or plastic bangles, which can be very attractive. She carries on wearing her gold ear-rings and rings on her fingers. Her feet and hands are often decorated in mendi (henna) on the wedding day.

Once she is married, she has to cover her head with the end of her sari when she is in front of her elders or miahsaab (moslem priest) (It is something I could not get used to!) Sometimes she greets them by touching their feet or kissing both cheeks (not always) and saying" Salaam Walay Kum".

It is customary that when the Bengali girl is married she is not allowed out of the house. She has to be accompanied by her inlaws when she wants to go shopping, etc. She is treated with care - after all a big dowry was paid for her! (A dowry is a sort of a down payment made by the bride's family to the bridegroom's family, for lasting security)

Before marriage from birth to teenage, in school days, or, if she is one of the lucky ones to further her education, she has to accompanied by an elder if she wants to go shopping or visiting relatives. It is unheard of for Bengali girls to go to discos or parties. Social gatherings are mostly with relatives. Seldom does she go out during the day.

She goes out early in the morning (often before sunrise) or late evening when it is dark. The men do the shopping and other errands. It is very unusual for a woman to be out during the day shopping. It was my first experience of this kind! Imagine not being able to walk on the road during the day as there was a line which women were not allowed to cross! I made the mistake of going out alone and all the women ran to tell me it was not allowed. We had to stay indoors.

However, one evening my mother-in-law and sister-in-law took me shopping at the local bazar. We went by rickshaw.

I felt a sense of freedom ; I was actually going out with the women! We went to several shops in the arcade and elswhere, looking for saris. The shop assistants were calling us to visit their shops to purchase saris at reasonable prices. We managed to buy a Jamdani sari at a discount price and left quite happy. We were given "pan" (beetle nut wrapped in the pan leaf) during the choosing of the saris ; as so many different colours were displayed. I found it difficult to choose as they all looked so beautiful.

Our next visit was to buy a pair of sandals from the shoe shop. There were many and we were invited by the assistants again. Eventually we bought a pair from the Bata shoe shop to match my black Jamdani sari. No discounts I am afraid to say!

It was nightfall by the time we were going home and as the rickshaw was passing along the Monu River, the sun was sinking in the horizon. It was a beautiful sunset. Travelling along Central road to our home, it was dusty and there were many people on the river bank.

The rickshaw drivers were busy taking people to and fro to their destinations. It was a smoky atmosphere. It was like a large room filled with smokers and everything very hazy. I felt a sense of security and also relief that the day was coming to an end. By the time we had arrived home it was very dark. It was time for a good cup of tea!

Living overseas and in my own country of Guyana I found it very difficult at first, but one can get used to the times one is not allowed out. The women in the city perhaps can move about more freely than the villagers and also as education amongst women is increasing. Perhaps in time they will be more free to go out as they wish to do.

Education amongst the Bengali women is still very limited, because of poverty, which one can agree is a vicious circle and one really has to hit the jackpot to get out of it. How often does one hit it ? Also because of the system of their society the girls are not allowed to further their education in modern studies. There must be some women who are brilliant but do not have the privelege of futhering their studies. I am so accustomed, living in Europe, to taking education for granted.

The education the girls are allowed is reading of the Koran and prayers (namaaz) which should be done five times a day in the Moslem community.

The Koran, a Moslem religious book, is the law for each individual Moslem to practice. The Hindus, Christians and other religions have their own method of teaching. It keeps people within the system which is really the law of the land. Once one has grasped any religion one is within the system and it helps one to re-think situations, before one does things that are considered wrong and not acceptable in the society in which one lives. It helps one to be a good person and to be helpful towards people especially the young and aged.

Religion is a never ending story and I was very privileged to witness the Durga Pooja in Moulvi Bazar. It lasts for three days and it is a festival everyone enjoys. The Durga Mataa (Mother) was a successful warrior in ancient times according to Hindu scriptures. Even today she is being worshipped by millions of Hindus throughout the world.

Most of the Bengali women are shy which results in difficulty in coping in many situations. For example, if the husband holds a professional job and invites his friends home, she might find it difficult to communicate, due to shyness and sometimes lack of education. It results in marital disagreement and the husband becomes very angry. Some of the husbands can be quite ignorant and cannot accept her for what she is but only for what he wants her to be, which is impossible!

When there is a problem between husband and wife, it involves all the relatives. Because of the arranged marriage the couple gets thorough counselling every time there is a problem between them. The bride and bridegroom can blame the person who arranged the marriage.

Banglar Bow has many sacrifices to make. Sometimes the husband resides abroad, most often in London. She has to wait for her entry permit, which could take up to three years or more. She is very lonely and gets depressed easily but is kept busy with the household chores. Lonliness comes at night when she retires to bed and cannot fall asleep and only thinks of her future life ahead, with her husband. She is desperate to change the situation she is living in, mostly the situation of poverty.

Balobasha or love is not to be discussed openly. It is a private affair. As I explained earlier, religion and custom play a great role in one's life. The respect level is high. Banglar Bow always has her head covered in front of men and elders.

Men play a dominant role in the Bengali society. It is totally a man's world in Bangladesh. The female's word is often of no value. Having said this about the Banglar Bow or female society in Bangladesh, the reader is probably aware that Bangladesh has a woman President, Begum Kaleda Azir. But I am writing mostly about the village women.

When reading this book I do not want them to feel they lack the intelligence of any other women in the world. They are intelligent but they have to live life as it is laid out for them, and poverty is a hard master. As a first time visitor in Bangladesh I am very happy to mention what I learned about their culture.

KALENGA

After a time I was beginning to feel bored and a little depressed because I am so accustomed to freedom in my life in Britain. My husband decided to take me for a midnight walk (which is forbidden to the women in this village) It was so dark I could not see where I was going because the very few street lamps were dimly lit. We decided to take a rickshaw to the bazar. It seemed as if I was the only woman out so late at night, I could only see men stairng at me. My husband mentioned to me that people do not have respect for women who are out late at night, but assured me he was not bothered.

I was surprised that most shops were still open after midnight. We were able to buy some apples and then returned home.

On our way home we questioned the rickshaw driver about his personal situation. I was interested to know his financial and family position. He told us he paid about thirty taka for rent of the rickshaw per day and took home about seventy taka per day if it was a good day. He was one of the fortunate ones not to have a large family to feed, only himself and his mother. We paid him well and gave him some apples (a luxury fruit in Bangladesh) as not many people can afford to buy them. He left full of appreciation and gratitude.

As it was a little cooler, we sat up most of the night talking, listened to the crickets, house lizards (they made a "tik - tik" noise), the dogs barking and the foxes howling -it sounded as if someone was in pain and I was quite scared. The mosquitoes had played a great role in our lives since we arrived-they never left us alone for a minute! Thanks to Boot's anti -stinging ointment we were relieved quickly of any burning itchiness. We slept with the portable electric fan blowing cool air over our warm bodies all night.

I found it difficult to get out of bed in the mornings, as our time difference is approximately six hours. By the time I was washed and dressed it was already nine o' clock in the morning or later sometimes, therefore I was subjected to dirty looks in the neighbourhood. They all got out of bed about six o' clock in the morning!

After a few days in Moulvi Bazar, we went to Kalenga; a remote place, about two miles from Moulvi Bazar. My husband had bought about four acres of land. It was very mountainous and full of fruit trees.

His main aim was to have an orphanage built so he took me along with some friends to see the beautiful scenery. We had to climb the mountain which was a little steep and I found it difficult to climb, as I was wearing sari and slippers. As I went further I could only think of my trainers and jeans. However we made it to the top and took some photographs. It was simply beautiful. Looking around we could only see green and a few houses down below. It was a gorgeous sunny day, and hot.

He bought this land a few years ago and built a small temporary house for a single mother and daughter, who take care of the land. The mother was very appreciative because she had no husband.

We went through the bumpy roads from Village Borkapon to Kalenga by rickshaw. The rickshaw is a bicycle stuck on a cart and ridden by a boy or man, who is usually half dead by the end of the day. As I climbed on the slanted seat and my husband sat besides me ; immediately I felt insecure. (There was a hood over our heads but we decided to leave it folded) When the rickshaw driver mounted his bicycle, I screamed ; I felt I was going to fall off the seat. This was my second time in the rickshaw. I was so tense I clutched the sides of the rickshaw. My husband kept saying "Relax", as he was accustomed to it and did not feel insecure. I believe there is a technique one has to master when sitting on the rickshaw and that is to use one's feet for pretending to brake when the rickshaw driver manoevres his vehicle!

Going through the dusty roads and lifting my head slowly I could see other people passing in their rickshaws, very carefree and not clutching the sides as I did; there were more rickshaws on the roads than cars or buses. They dominated the roads, I would say, like the black cabs in London. The rickshaw drivers feel they have more rights on the roads than any other drivers (after all they are the lowest paid workers).

The road from Village Borkpon to Kalenga was very bumpy and was full of pot holes and ramps. In some streets there was no tarmacadam. The roads and streets were very sandy and full of dust. We had to cover our nostrils and mouths for the fear of inhaling half of the roadside!

There were some shops and houses on the way to Kalenga. Some of the houses were magnificent and painted white which made them look even more grand. I fell in love with one particular house on the way. Because it was so huge and painted white it was like a dream house, but the road it overlooked was in an appalling condition.

There were many fruit, coconut, beetle nut (supari) trees. They added colour to the picture. The men were dressed in longi (similiar to a long skirt) and shirt or kurta and the women wore saris or shalwar kameez.

There were people constantly chewing the beetle nut mixed with pan leaf and sometimes tune (a white substance, powdery in texture) added. It is a delicacy and very good for indigestion. The only problem is it ruins one's teeth; therefore most of the Bengali community has extremely bad teeth. When they smiled one could see very dark red teeth which were sometimes broken. I must say it is nothing to admire! Often the lips are stained dark red.

That was the end of another hot sunny day! We returned home about two o' clock in the afternoon to have lunch only to discover a leech on the kitchen floor. My mother-in-law told Siddeck, one of the family members, to dispose of it discreetly.

After a good lunch I noticed blood on my sari and went into the bedroom to investigate further, only to discover I had brought the two little devils from Kalenga! They had a good drink because when I lifted my sari, I could see the blood dripping from my left leg and left upper thigh. I was hysterical because I could not undo the string from my petticoat

(I immediately remembered the horror movies I had seen and the actresses in the same position as I was) I used a pair of scissors which were handy to cut the string. I immediately took a dettol bath, head to toes as I felt there must be more all over. The feeling is indescribable.

All the women in the neighbourhood came to investigate what was going on and had a little look, frowned and left. Oh, well it is my leg! Something to gossip about! As I explained earlier on, privacy is very limited.

BROMON

Talking about privacy, when we first arrived in Village Borkapon on our first morning, we were woken by some ravens (Kowa) What a noise! Kow! Kow! It sounded as if someone was saying, "Eat, eat," because in Bengali "Kow" means to eat! It really disturbed my brain cells! It was if there were fire-works going on in my brain. I could not get used to those birds.

In the house where we stayed, there was no kitchen, only a large bedroom and bathroom. (We had all meals in our other bungalow) We had quite a large sitting room with a television, settee, a few chairs and a couch. It was very simple and spacious. We had a portable fan.

Sometimes I watched Bangladesh programmes or if we were lucky we had Indian programmes on the television. The women in the neighbourhood always sat with me in the evenings. We watched television and tried to communicate. Although I am brown - skinned, I cannot speak Bengali. I understood most of the conversation but found it difficult to make sentences. They had a good laugh at my Bengali as I had at their English!

Most of the houses in the Village were bungalows made from brick. There were a few thatched roofs and mud walled houses.

When I entered our other house, to have breakfast, it was mostly tea and toast. I found the eggs too strong and whenever I ate one I felt nauseated afterwards.

Most of the kitchens have a two burner gas cooker. The Bengali kitchen is very different from a European kitchen, just two long shelves, one to hold all the kitchen utensils and another for the cooker. There is a sink and tap water from the overhead tank that is filled from the artesian well, by using an electric pump.

Most of the washing is done in the pond (muddy pool) as most people tended to have their own ponds. They bathed, washed their utensils, clothes, vegetables and all other cooking items.

As our time was very limited, we had to make the best of it.

Our next journey was to another remote town called Shomshu Nugger. It was on a well chosen pre - arranged day. We went with some relatives. We packed as much to eat as we could because it was a long journey. We went by mini - bus, nine of us altogether.

Because of pot holes in the roads we were diverted through Banugas, towards Sri Mongol, then Shomshu Nugger. The scenery was unbelievable ; one would have thought that one was in Europe. It was quite mountainous on both sides of the road and the green trees were sparkling from the sunshine. It was a very hot and humid day. We passed many tea estates and rice fields. The women were quite busy picking tea leaves.

We had to cross a number of bridges. Because they were so narrow I thought we would capsize. When I looked out of the window of the mini - bus, below the bridges, the rivers were half dried. There were men dressed in longi wrapped as loin cloths (rolled upwards towards the upper thighs and fastened between the inner thighs) collecting sand for construction of the roads.

It was nearly 3 o' clock in the afternoon when we arrived at our hosts' residence. Naturally we had not telephoned, as it was very difficult to make any connections with the telephone, but automatically we were accepted and a cooked meal was provided for us. We ate well because we had not had our snacks.

They wanted us to stay but as our time in Bangladesh was limited we left about 5 o' clock in the evening.

It was a beautiful village and the people were warm and welcoming. They liked us and we liked them. The houses were similiar to where we were staying. The fan was there to keep us cool.

Our return journey was on the same road, only now it was getting dark. The sunset was beautiful. When we arrived home there was a power cut. Another one! Not for long, always short ones. The mosquitoes were welcoming! Oh, well, it was a good day!

When we first arrived in Moulvi Bazar, I fished nearly everyday. I loved to go fishing, especially when the fishes were playing with the bait. I screamed with joy every time I pulled the rod and there was a fish dangling. It was a good feeling! Our pond was beautifully surrounded by sucker, mango and lychee trees.

The best time to go fishing was early morning and evening. That was the time they seemed to come out from their shelter. Once I caught three Shoals (Shoal is the name of a Bengali fish) and we made them into chutney, which was delicious!

In between my fishing we had a tremendous number of guests. Although my Bengali is minimal,

I did try to communicate but found myself frustrated at times. I did not have an interpreter because my husband was busy with his friends. There was another family a few doors away, from Britain, so I could speak English with them.

Although most days were hot and sunny, I found, after washing my clothes, they were not drying as I expected because of the humidity. I was not allowed to do any household chores or cooking but I insisted and did some. I had to do some work because in Britain I do all my own housework and gardening.

I swept the floor in our house, using a broom made from the beetle nut tree. The outside of the house was swept with a broom made from coconut branches. I had to mop the floor every day because of the dust and sand. I enjoyed doing the work and the people found it amazing that I could actually work! Also I did not want to get bored because we were visiting relatives and places. I was considered a new bride or bow because it was my first visit to Bangladesh (after being married for so long!) We had continual rain for three days and nights, during the Durga Pooja. I was told it was normal for rain to come on such an auspicious occasion, otherwise the Mother Durga was not pleased with the people. We had to stay indoors but I did not find it boring. We made some gulab jamun sweets. We also watched television and had endless conversations.

Our dog, Lotus was dying. I have never witnessed such pain as that animal went through! It cried, writhed with pain and foamed from the mouth. Poor dog! It was throwing itself anywhere and at anybody's door step. One man took a stick and violently shoved it from his door step, into the mud and poked it into another area. I felt dreadful but he has children and the dog was dying from rabies. It was raining and cold. The dog was shivering. It had lost a lot of weight and one could count the ribs.

We could not bear the crying from the dog any longer and called the local veterinary surgeon, which was quite unusal, we were told, because normally the locals leave the animals to die, although they are suffering. My husband and I felt it more because we are dog lovers and owners.

Eventually the veterinary surgeon's assistant came and injected the dog with a chemical that induced a massive heart attack. It was the midday assan (prayers) and Lotus was laid to rest peacefully. The men dug a deep hole by the front pond and buried him. It was an experience I shall never forget!

After fifteen days, my visa was expired. As mentioned earlier we went to the local "S.P." office in Moulvi Bazar; by rickshaw. It was a small building but well guarded. The day was hot and humid.

On arrival at the " S.P." office we were told it was the wrong office and we should go to the passport office in Sylhet. The "S.P." officer, a very dark skinned man was more concerned about my religion than my visa. There was a very heated conversation between him and my husband, concerning my religion. He turned the pages of my passport many times. He felt I should have converted to a moslem but my husband assured him it was not a problem between us because religion is an individual's responsibility. I understood most of the coversation as it was Bengali but did not speak a word and left. We both felt humilated because of the attitude of the officer. We felt mentally disturbed.

Having rested well, we were up early the next day, breakfasted, showered and got ready for another journey. We had planned to visit as many places as possible in the short time we were there.

Our mini-bus was parked under a tree, near the large pond in front of the house. Six of us were going. It was nearly 10' o clock in the morning and it was hot and uncomfortable. On every journey we took snacks and mineral water.

We were on our way to the tea estate. Our first stop was at the local hospital in Moulvi Bazar, a government building. I wanted to see the hospital wards and whether they were exactly like the pictures seen on television in Britain.

It was a huge two - storeyed building and the white paint was peeling from the walls. We went up a large staircase to the top floor ward. On our way up there were blood stained walls and piles of dust left in corners of the stairs. There was an obnoxious smell in the hospital.

We had no appointment but went into the ward, where we could see the doctor examining the patients openly. I spoke to the doctor and was asking him some questions about the patients as I am a qualified nurse. He said because of illiteracy most of the patients lacked good hygiene care, resulting in unnecessary illnesses.

It was a forty- bedded ward we visited and it was exactly as seen on the television in Britain. The bed linen was filthy, black from dirt and some patients slept on bare mattresses that were also black. There was no overhead oxygen or suction like we have in British hospitals. Minimum equipment was provided for use in the hospitals because, as the good doctor explained, Bangladesh is a very poor country. The government cannot afford to provide sufficient funds for patient care.

The doctors and nurses work very long hours, often without breaks and are low paid. There were about four doctors to run this hospital that held about one hundred beds and they also had to work in casualty.

There were only two cleaners in the whole of Moulvi Bazar General hospital. That was why most of the dirt was swept and left in a suitable corner. A vacuum cleaner is unheard of; brooms are used to sweep the floor.

We thanked the doctor and left.

Our next visit was to the tea estate called Bangladesh National Tea. It was pre- arranged for us to visit the beautiful tea gardens, the leaves of the tea trees were different shades of green.

It was a joy to watch the women with large baskets on their backs and straw hats picking the tea leaves. The tea garden was on the outskirts of Moulvi Bazar. There were also other tea estates owned by other companies.

We went to the Manager's house, a beautiful white - painted bungalow, situated on top of the hill, where we were entertained with tea and biscuits before being taken to the plantation and the tea factory.

As our mini-bus made its way up the steep slope towards the foothills of the mountains where the tea plants were grown, I again felt very insecure, as if our mini-bus would capsize.

The tea leaves were very dark green and the plants were bushy. I managed a few photographs of ourselves picking the tea leaves. I was hesitant at first, to get in amongst the bushes, because of my bad experience in Kalenga, with the leeches! Without encouragement I would not have done so!

At the end of the day the tea pickers took their leaves to the tea factory where the leaves are weighed by kilograms. They are then paid according to the kilograms picked. The leaves are washed and dried in huge dryers at a certain temperature. After several hours of drying they are taken into a different building to be crushed and dried further. Different flavours and grades are made, then packed into large wooden crates ready for shipment overseas. I believe the leaves were auctioned to various business men, who took the leaves to the nearest port, mostly Chittagong, to be transported all over the world.

The tea plantation we visited was approximately twelve hundred acres and had about seven hundred employees. It was a small business in comparison to the other plantations.

At the end of our visit we were given three different flavours, as samples to be taken home. I was looking forward to sharing them with my friends in Britain.

We also visited the Bangladesh tea research centre but were not allowed in the laboratory. However we walked around the tea gardens and took some photographs amongst the fully grown tea trees that were used for seed to be grown into new plants. Surrounding the research centre were a variety of flowering plants and trees, there were mostly hibiscus - pink, red and white.

It was already 2 o'clock in the afternoon and it was hot and humid. Our next visit was to the cholera clinic in Raj Nugger, on the outskirts of Moulvi Bazar. It was up on a hill. On the way we passed the leprosy clinic but did not visit it. We went into the cholera clinic which was clean and well kept. The accountant, who worked at the clinic, was a friend of one of our guides and once again we were treated with great hospitality and welcomed to his house.

The clinic was situated in a beautiful secluded place, surrounded by flowers and trees. However, because it was in a remote area there was no gas for cooking, only clay cookers that used wood for fuel. We were told exactly the same as the doctor in Moulvi Bazar General Hospital had told us. Due to illiteracy most patients lacked good hygiene care and as a consequence suffered from all kinds of diseases.

Cholera is a bacterial infection of man caused by Vibrio cholerae (of classical or El Tor biotypes) which characteristically causes severe diarrhoea, and death (in those severally affected) from water and electrolyte depletion. Spread is directly from person to person by the faecal - oral route, or indirectly by infected food or water. It can spread to any part of the world, and become endemic where standards of environmental sanitation and personal hygiene are low. Man is the only reservoir of infection. The El Tor biotype has now largely displaced classical cholera as the major pathogen of public health importance.

After an incubation period usually in the range 1-5 days, profuse painless diarrhoea follows. The diarrhoea is typically watery, white, and flecked with mucus, the infamous 'rice-water stool'. In 80% of cases, vomiting follows soon after diarrhoea. Fever is unusual except in children, and short-lived. There is no significant inflammation of the gut.

Dehydration is caused by the profuse diarrhoea, compounded by the usual inability to retain fluids by mouth. The speed with which severe dehydration occurs is greater than any other disease.

Rehydration is the mainstay of cholera treatment. In severe cases the restoration of blood volume is urgently needed, and this can only be achieved rapidly by intravenous infusion. Simpler methods such as oral rehydration can be used with results almost as good, certainly in adults.

Cholera vaccine has no significant part to play in controlling the disease. Vaccination gives perhaps 50 % immunity for up to 6 months, but the infection, when it does develop in the vaccinated, is not of reduced severity.

The day was almost closing and we were now moving to Kalenga. I was petrified to go because of the leeches. We wanted to see the workmens' progress in slicing the top of the mountain for the building of the orphanage. Our mini-bus was stuck in the middle of the sandy road because there was a large pot hole! It was time to show the greatest strength amongst the men and, by jove they lifted it out! It took quite a few men from the village. They were dressed in vests and longees.

We took photographs of the work that was done by the men. The local residents turned up to see us off as if we were celebrities! We had to walk quite a distance because we had been stuck in a pot hole earlier. All aboard! We were on our way home again! It was a black night. We were ready to eat anything and I was ready for a good night's sleep although it was only 8 'o clock in the evening. Oh yes, and no attacks from leeches!

It was one visit after another for the short period we were in Bangladesh. Another day three of us went to Sylhet, two and a half hours away from Moulvi Bazar over a rough pot - holed road.

We passed many wedding decorations, tea estates and ricefields.

When we arrived in the town centre it was a different scene altogether. I have never seen such a chaotic town! A road about twenty or thirty yards wide had approximately a six - way system and it was only meant to be a two way system. Rickshaws, baby taxis, bicycles, cars and lorries - everyone seemed to want to get passed at the same time.

It was most uncomfortable sitting waiting in the mini - bus for the traffic to clear. The perspiration was pouring down our well clad bodies ; wearing the sari did not help much! We lost our tempers many times as we could not move an inch because of the constipated traffic. We were stuck for hours in one place. As our chauffeur forced his way along, I felt he deserved a medal! He was marvellous. No one could have done better.

One little incident happened on the way just before we entered the town. our chauffeur was suddenly stopped by the traffic police, who demanded one hundred taka. He had no choice but to make the payment to the officer or else a fault would have been made on his vehicle, which would have resulted in a fine.

It is a must for all visitors to go to the Shazalal tomb in Sylhet, so we went there. We took' Prasad' and fed the beggars. I was told wishes came true if one visited the tomb. I made mine but was told women were prohibited from going upstairs where the tomb was - only men were allowed. I felt my wishes were not accepted ; I felt distant from the Emperor Shazalal. I stood at the bottom of the stairs with my hands open like a beggar's, helpless but wishing for my dreams to come true. I was not satisfied because of the distance! We went to the well and made more wishes but I felt disappointed and left. I was sure the law was man - made that women were forbidden to go upstairs to the tomb. My heart felt the great Emperor Shazalal would not have discriminated between the sexes. I hope, one day, the law will change and women can visit the tomb.

There were huge pots where donations were made by the visitors ; the money, I was told, fed the numerous beggars.

The Emperor Shazalal was a great man because he led most of the Hindus into the teaching of Islam. It resulted in most Hindus being converted into Moslems. Most Bangladeshis are ex -Hindus.

Oh yes I had to wear my assel, the end piece of my sari over my head! It was meant to be a mark of respect, so no escaping for me as I did previously.

We bought agarbatti and attar (incense and perfume) and left.

It was another long journey home and it was dark except for another beautiful sunset. The crimson sun was so large ; it cast a wonderful variety of colours on Mother Earth. It was like a painting with all the rich colours - orange, gold and ruby. It was sad to see it disappear into the horizon. I shall never forget the colour of the ricefields, transformed with these different shades.

I was so tired that I fell asleep for a little while on the way home and then it was time for a shower, dinner and another dream!

The heat often very humid, and the long journeys were very exhausting and for our next few days we stayed quietly at home entertaining friends and relatives. We did manage a few last visits, locally, to relatives.

I was given many saris as gifts because I was the new bride.

In between entertaining, I was washing and ironing our clothes. On the last day I had a little tea party. We bought lots of sweets from the local shops. They were delicious. I could live happily in an Asian sweet shop! My tea party was a success ; I had all the seniors and juniors. What a ball! The music vibrated the walls of the house but no one danced. As I explained earlier, the culture is totally different from western society. In Bangladesh the respect level is higher.

In the evening, I had my hands painted with the henna paint (the fresh leaves were picked and crushed) and placed on the back and palm of my hands and fingers. I had to wait for one uncomfortable hour before the crushed leaves were removed and what beautiful patterns they were, especially on my fingers. My sister-in-law was quite proud of her artistic values in creating such patterns.

Well I made my home for four weeks, in Village Borkapon. The parting was painful. During my stay I had so much love and affection showered on to me it reminded me of my own country, Guyana, when I was a little girl. I had so much affection from everyone I left feeling like a little girl. It was a wonderful feeling!

DESHAY PEERA

On 26th October, 1991, about 7.30 in the morning we left Village Borkapon with two suitcases well packed. One suitcase was packed with all my saris and the other with dried fishes, vegetables and a few other parcels for relatives residing in Britain.

The whole village had turned up ; it was quite a scene. There was a long queue of women whom I kissed gooodbye. It was an emotional time I would have liked to avoid, especilly with my in-laws. I had warned my mother-in-law the previous night not to cry too much, when we would leave. It sounded very callous but I could not accomodate any more tears.

Our mini-bus was waiting for us in front of the house by the pond. As we walked towards the vehicle, everyone followed us. My heart was grieving to leave them but I was happy to return to our home in Scotland. It seemed as if everyone had a fixed stare at us, as we were leaving, trying to keep our picture in their hearts.

We went to Sri Mongol station, for the 8 o' clock train but it was late by ten minutes. We were taken to the station by my husband's cousin and a friend.

The station was over-crowded with people. Most were waiting for the train, some of them selling cigarettes and other items. The station was swarming with mendicants. It was a very sunny morning.

I felt very sad when we were leaving the two men at the station. I stood on the steps of the train talking to my husband's cousin. He could not speak English and my Bengali was not very good. He tried to give me some money but I refused it. All I said was "Kudavis Baisaab" "God be with you brother". The train started to move and I waved to him. I felt my tears and I could see his.

We were soon settled. This time it was a different first class carriage ; we had tables infront of us and there were a lot more people. There were fans and overhead racks that we used for our suitcases. One gentleman sat infront of us throughout our journey.

We were on our way to Dhaka, to visit a few places before we returned home. Our flight was in the evening of the 29th October, so we had about three days left.

It was another long journey and I had not had a good breakfast. I was a little hungry but would not eat or drink anything. I thought I would wait until we arrived in Dhaka and on the journey I started writing this book because my experiences in Moulvi Bazar were still fresh.

We fell asleep part of the journey because the previous night we had not slept. My husband had sat up all night talking to his relations and I had tried to sleep but failed. Their voices were quite high pitched! They kindly gave him one hour to himself and he tried to rest in that hour. By the time he was settled there was a loud bang on the door for us to get dressed. And that was about 5.30 in the morning!

Our first stop was Nuafara and what a commotion in the train - two policemen were chasing a young lad who was in our carriage. In seconds he jumped out the window of the train and made a run for it. I do not know how he did it because he was wearing longi and vest!

We made several stops along the way and as usual the men sold their fruits, chocolates, cigarettes, etc.

Another excitement was when the train stopped at Akaura. It appeared the whole village was there! There were people shouting and cheering and of course we were all curious to know what was the event. It was a film actor who had visited his relatives and was now returning to Dhaka. Also in our carriage were a few members of parliament.

It was a suuny day. We passed a few rivers on the way that made me feel thirsty and I could only think of a long swim. Our journey ended and we arrived in Dhaka, about 2.30 in the afternoon.

Kamplapur station was chaotic as usual. A porter took our luggage to a taxi. It was such a humid day!

We stayed at the Hotel Purbani until our departure date, a large hotel situated in the heart of Dhaka and overlooking statues of flamingoes.

After we had checked in, we had a meal in our room. We were both extremely hungry. You would not guess what happened to me after the meal! Yes, the same as when I first went to Moulvi Bazar - vomiting and diarrhoea. I was ill, I could not breathe, but we were not allowed to open the windows because the building was air conditioned and also for security reasons. I felt claustrophobic, I had to go out for fresh air but where would I get it ? It was a hot day and the air was unpleasant. I returned to our room and ordered saline water to drink. My entire evening was spent nursing myself feeling miserable and sorry for myself, dozing and wakening. About 11.30 in the evening, we went for a little walk. We thought the air would be fresher but it was no different. We were not too far from the hotel, when we noticed a few of the hotel staff had followed us to warn us not to venture too far, because we might fall prey to some hooligans. We returned to the hotel and again I was sick. Eventually I went to sleep. It was an eventful day and a trying day!

Next morning, I woke up and felt well again. We had a large breakfast and contacted our friends Badal and Gillian, who were also on holiday from Scotland. In no time he was in our hotel to show us around Dhaka, as Badal was born and bred in Dhaka.

Badal took us to his house, which was not too far from the hotel Purbani. Gillian was sitting on their veranda waiting for us. She looked beautiful in her Shalwar Kameez. We met the rest of the family. They greeted us warmly and fed us, as usual, a number of different Bengali dishes. It is traditional to serve guests with all the different bhagees, curries and rice. And the guests always take sweets, like Ras Malai and Burphi. After our meal we went shopping.

We went with the baby taxi but we had to use our handkerchiefs to cover our mouths and nostrils. What fumes and what chaotic traffic!

We went to a number of shops, I was impressed with the shop called "Aarong" because it had everything one needed. We purchased a few things then returned to Badal and Gillian's residence. It was 8 'o clock in the evening. We refreshed ourselves and were collected by another friend, Baboo, who took us for a Thai meal at one of the local restaurants. After a delicious meal we returned to our hotel.

Next day Badal and Gillian collected us about 11 'o clock in the morning and we went on another shopping adventure. It was great! We spent the entire day in the city. (Although Bangladesh is considered one of the poorest of third world nations ; there were no food shortages and the fashion industry was at its' peak)

We parted company and returned to our hotel. It was time for quick showers and our meal - a buffet dinner. We tried almost everything but I would recommend the curried Hilsha (Bangladesh National Fish)

Tuesday 29th October, our day to return home. Badal and Gillian collected us, we took two rickshaws as I believed it was more safe to ride on a rickshaw than a car! But my little heart was pumping away, with fright. The rickshaw drivers were the masters of the roads. I was still clutching the sides of the rickshaw! However, we went to visit our previous hosts, who took care of us when we first arrived in Bangladesh, Mr. & Mrs. Shafiq Ur - Rahman and family. It was delightful to see them and the children. Another Chinese meal and and soon it would be time to part company.

After collecting and paying our bills, we left. Mr. Shafiq Ur - Rahman, Gillian and Badal took us to the Airport. Our flight was leaving at 8.50 in the evening.

After we had checked in at the British Airways counter and were left with just our hand luggage we went outside to thank our friends for taking care of us. We had about half an hour to chat. It was a cool night because the winter in Bangladesh was just beginning.

During the time we stood outside, chatting, the recollections of my holiday were still fresh. I felt sad and happy. I had had a good holiday and was so well treated where ever I went that I felt I was at home in my own country. The people were warm and friendly.

At about 9.15, we parted company. I felt sad to leave them.

We had an unpleasant experience at the immigration desk when the immigration officer kept us waiting behind all the others, then had a heated argument with my husband, demanding a bribe because my visa had not been renewed. I became really upset when he ordered our luggage out of the aircraft and, crying, asked to see his Superintendent. He, good man, saved the situation, got my passport stamped and we were on board in no time. But it was an experience I will not forget!

We said farewell to Zia International Airport, farewell Bangladesh until we return again.

As I was about to fall asleep, I kept remembering my wonderful experiences in Bangladesh and the happy and unhappy times Babul and I had over the years. Now we were returning home to a fresh start and hopefully pleasant situations ahead.

We arrived in London Heathrow Airport at about 5.10 in the morning. It was a good thirteen hours' flight. It was very cold in London. We took a taxi and returned to our previous hosts Mr. & Mrs. Sattar in Horndean. We stayed overnight and once again was happy to see the children.

After a good breakfast we thanked our hosts and left. It was a long drive for my husband. (I shall never forget the scenery from London to Scotland) It was autumn and the leaves on the trees were absolutely golden, bronze, red and orange.

It took us about eleven hours to reach our home in Balloch, Inverness. The dogs were well looked after by Mr. Allan and my husband's younger brother, Jahangir. Well done lads!

We were cold and tired. We were happy to go to bed and the dogs soon joined us!

When I go from hence let this be my parting word,
that what I have seen is unsurpassable.

I have tasted of the hidden honey of this lotus that
expands on the ocean of light, and thus am I blessed
Gitanjali (Rabindranath Tagore)

ABOUT THE AUTHOR

I was born at No. 47 Village, Corentyne, Berbice, Guyana; South America at my maternal grand parents' home and brought up at Fyrish Road. Most of my father's relatives lived at Fyrish Village. My paternal grand parents lived at Palmyra. They had bought a colonial style home which was owned by a Manager who worked at the Sugar Plantation.Guyana was a British Colony until 1966 when it had gained its independence. The Manager returned to Great Britain in the late 1950's and left all their antique furniture which included their four poster beds. I used to love going there as a child to admire their bathroom and beds.

When we were growing up we could not get into any trouble because the neighbours were also responsible for our care.

I came to Britain in 1971 to pursue my career in Nursing and achieved a lot of qualifications. I am currently working as a Pre-admission Sister at a London Hospital. I have received the Chairman's Award 2002 and 2005 for 'Most Caring Individual'. We have a yearly event at my hospital whereby the Chairman acknowledges the hard work we do. I have also been awarded 'Nominee Nurse of the Year' 2006. I enjoy caring for people.

I enjoy travelling and have travelled to quite a few countries; trying to balance my working life in this short life can be stressful at times!

I love painting and I am a water colour artist. I have done exhibitions when I was living in Scotland. Every year we hired a hall to do our exhibition when each member is allowed to diplay four paintings.

I enjoy writing and I have been doing so since as a child but I have only published through magazines in the past.

www.ingramcontent.com/pod-product-compliance
Lightning Source LLC
Chambersburg PA
CBHW031325290526
45784CB00014B/2136